DOCTOR Li
AND THE CROWN-WEARING VIRUS

BY **FRANCESCA CAVALLO**

ILLUSTRATED BY **CLAUDIA FLANDOLI**

EDITORIAL DIRECTOR: Francesca Cavallo
ART DIRECTOR: Samuele Motta

STORY: Francesca Cavallo
EDITOR: Anita Roy

ILLUSTRATIONS: Claudia Flandoli

ISBN 978-1-953592-00-2

Doctor Li and the Crown-wearing Virus is the first
book published by Undercats, Inc.

It is unusual for a children's book to tackle such
difficult topics. But at Undercats, we believe
children's books are opportunities for families to
come together, to look at the world as it is and to
imagine what it could become.

If you want us to keep you posted about our
upcoming releases sign up at

www.undercats.com

Dear Reader,

I don't know about you, but to me, so far, 2020 has felt strange and unreal – like living through a fairy-tale. At this point, it feels like I'm somewhere in the deep, dark woods, where everything is possible and most of it is out of my control.

The pandemic has brought a lot of uncertainty into my life. I left my home abruptly. I was unable to see my friends or family because of the lockdown. While I was in isolation, all I could think was "What can I do?", "How can I help?"

I sat down and wrote a story to help children understand what was going on. I put it up on my website, and something magical happened: tens of thousands of people downloaded it and volunteers from every corner of the globe translated it into more than 30 languages. That amazing response gave me the courage to turn that little experiment into the book you're holding in your hands right now.

The pandemic made me feel lost and fearful at times. But writing and sharing this story helped me realize that I was not alone – and neither are you.

We will find our way out of the deep, dark woods in the end. And when we finally do, depending on the way we behaved while we felt lost and afraid, we will have discovered something important about ourselves and about the world.

May, the seven-year-old girl in this story, made three amazing discoveries.

I cannot wait to find out what yours will be.

With love,
Francesca Cavallo

To Doctor Li's children
and to the brave children of the world -

As you build the future of our planet
May you always remember
This extraordinary time
When we found out
That we do not walk alone

That when one of us falls
We all fall

And when one of us rises
We all rise.

DOCTOR Li

AND THE CROWN-WEARING

VIRUS

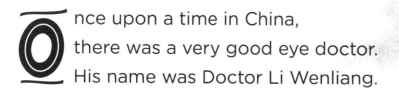

Once upon a time in China,
there was a very good eye doctor.
His name was Doctor Li Wenliang.

Every day, Doctor Li saw his patients
in the Central Hospital of a big city called Wuhan.

Doctor Li treated people who all had different
problems with their eyesight. Some needed
eyedrops to stop their eyes itching. Some needed
an operation. Some just needed new glasses.

He took care of everyone with joy.

One day, though, Doctor Li began to notice that more and more of the patients in his waiting room had something else wrong with them. It was not just their eyes: they complained of fevers, headaches and a strange, dry cough that wouldn't go away.

He wondered what was going on. When Doctor Ai Fen, the head of the hospital's emergency department, came to see him, he asked her about it.

"It's a coronavirus," she told him, "and it's very contagious. At least seven people have already fallen ill."

"We must tell everyone to wear protective gear immediately! Otherwise they'll get the virus from their patients and it will spread out of control," said Doctor Li, and he sent an urgent message to all his colleagues.

Doctor Li was at home that evening when suddenly there was a loud banging on the door. He jumped up. It was the police.

"Are you Doctor Li Wenliang?" demanded one officer, frowning.
"Yes, ma'am," answered the doctor, looking at her, a little scared.
"You must stop spreading all these lies about a new virus in Wuhan," the other policeman said.

"But I'm not lying!" protested Doctor Li.
"If you don't stop, we'll throw you in jail. Sign here."

And they forced him to sign a letter saying that he was wrong and was making a fuss over nothing. They did the same with Doctor Ai Fen. "You must not say a word to anyone about this," they told her, "not even your husband."

But every day more and more ill people were admitted to the hospital in Wuhan. And, since they were not wearing protective gear, the doctors and nurses who worked there started to fall ill too, just as Doctor Li had feared.

On January 10th 2020, Doctor Li started coughing. He got a fever and realized he couldn't taste the tea he was drinking. These were all symptoms of Covid-19, the illness caused by the new virus.

"I can't stay silent while people are falling sick. I have to do something," thought Doctor Li.

Although he was scared of being sent to prison, he started to tell everyone about the virus, and about the police trying to silence him.

Doctor Li's words flew far beyond his hospital room in Wuhan to every corner of China, and soon reached the whole world.

A dangerous virus was going around and the police were threatening the doctors who were trying to fight it? The people of China raised their voices in protest: "We want freedom! Long live Doctor Li!"

The protests got louder and louder until the authorities were forced to back down. They apologized to Doctor Li – but by then it was too late.

The doctor's illness got worse,
and on February 7th 2020, he died.

May and her mom Laura were at home on the other side of the world when they heard the news. May was sad to hear about Doctor Li and Laura worried about the way the virus was spreading in the United States too.

"What is a virus, mom?" May asked.

"It's an infectious agent that is so tiny you can only see it with a microscope. 'Infectious' means that, even though it's so small, it can make people, animals and even plants very ill," her mom explained.

"Why is the President saying the virus doesn't exist?"

Laura paused. "Sometimes," she said, "when there is a very big problem, people get scared and think that if they pretend the problem isn't there, it will just disappear."

"Are we going to get the virus like Doctor Li?" worried May.

"I don't know, May," Laura said, "but lots of scientists are studying the situation. How about we find out together what they've discovered so far?"

May nodded enthusiastically. She loved learning new things with her mom.

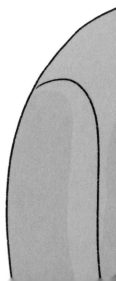

That afternoon, May and her mom discovered a lot!

• The virus is called 'coronavirus' because under the microscope it looks like it is wearing a crown, and 'corona' is Latin for crown.

• The virus – almost certainly – came from a bat.

- It is rare for a virus to hop from an animal to humans, but this one had made it!

- Even if you're not ill, you can still pass on the virus to others! That's why Doctor Li wanted everyone to wear a mask.

- The virus disappears from your hands if you wash them really well with soap.

- Protecting wild animals from close contact with humans makes it much harder for diseases like this to spread.

"Here," said Laura one afternoon, holding out a facemask.
"Put this on and we can go see your grandparents. I've got one too!"

When they arrived, May wanted to give her grandpa a hug. "Haven't you heard?" he joked. "We have 'corona-free' greetings now!" And he stood on one leg and waggled his foot at her. May laughed.

But she and her mother noticed other people were not wearing masks or keeping a safe distance from each other.

In fact, the virus kept on being passed from person to person.

When too many people fell ill, all the schools in the world – including May's - closed down to slow the spread of infection.

All of a sudden, everyone had to stay at home, and people were only allowed out to buy food and medicine. Gyms, hairdressers, movie theaters and pools closed, and beaches and parks stood empty.

In the beginning, not going to school was fun. May could wake up late and - since her mom was working from home - they could be together all day long. They baked cookies and played a lot because doing lessons online took way less time than going to school.

One night, though, May sat on her bed trying to listen to her feelings. She stared at her school bag that she did not need to pack, and she felt sad. She realized how much she missed her friends and her teachers. Birthday parties just weren't the same on Zoom: it wasn't fun to see gifts being unwrapped through the screen and she didn't get to taste any of her friends' birthday cakes.

She gazed out of her window and realized that her neighbors were sad too. Even her mom, who was usually always smiling, looked worried.

It was then that she spotted the colored pencils on her desk. She thought about Doctor Li and she said to herself, "I have to do something."

So she drew a gigantic rainbow and hung it out of her window.

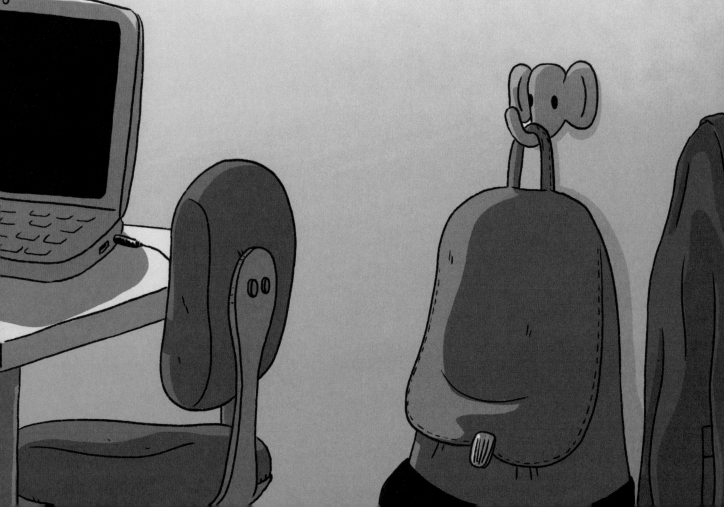

In the morning, the couple next door saw May's rainbow. "How wonderful!" they said. "We want to do something too." So they baked a huge cake and gave a slice to everyone in their building – including Johnny, a homeless man who was passing by. Three of her neighbors leaned out of their windows and started playing music together. An old lady sat with her window wide open and read out stories for all the kids to enjoy.

Just like Doctor Li's words, May's rainbow soon reached every corner of the globe. Children hung beautiful rainbows outside their windows to remind people how important it was to take care of each other. Everyone started to wear facemasks and to wash their hands carefully with soap. People made up their own corona-free greetings. As long as everyone was careful, the virus didn't spread as easily anymore.

Slowly, buses started running again and schools reopened.

Meeting friends again after all that time felt strange at first and then amazing!

"So, what did you learn over the past few months?" May's teacher, Mr. Lewis, asked the class when they finally got back together.

"I learned how to make bread!" said Henri.

"I learned that vaccines are super important to protect people from diseases. And when I grow up, I want to be a great scientist," said Emily.

"I planted five trees," Thomas told everyone. "And when I grow up, I will protect the planet. I will save forests so wild animals have a safe place to live, far away from humans, and nasty viruses won't force us to close schools anymore."

"And what did *you* learn, May?" asked Mr. Lewis.

May thought hard. "I learned three things," she said. "One is that I want to become President to make sure all grandparents are happy and healthy, and that brave people like Doctor Li are free. Two is that when there is a big problem, you can't hide from it. You need to be brave and face it, even when it's scary."

"And three?" asked all of her classmates in one voice.

"Three is that even when we're on our own, we're all connected. If one of us rises, we all do. Because it's not just viruses that are contagious," she said, "rainbows are too!"

What did *you* learn during the pandemic?

The Bravest of the Brave

This book would have not been made if it weren't for the support of an international community of 1,322 backers on Kickstarter. Thank you!

Below, you'll find a special dedication to a few small and big heroes of this pandemic.

Ivan Canu and Mimaster Illustrazione
Giulia and Matteo Rossi
Sara and Emanuela
李庆珍 (Li Qingzhen) and 李书起 (Li Shuqi)
Meiwen Chen and Rachèl Harmsen
Ying Zhang and Ce Ji
Nonno Calzà Tomaso and Nonna Calzà Minatti Riccarda
Giulia Ruffilli and Susan Silbermann
Paloma Maria and Lucia Valentina Torres-Slavik
Matteo Riccardi and Paola Frattola
Adriano
Tatiana
The Ostenso-Taipale and the Odham families
Maria 意安 and Hongmei
George and Andrew Horng
Mattia and Samuele Schenatti
Andrea and Emily DiFederico
Oliver J. and Meghan Harrison
Bram Otto Cantrall-Mintzer
Yang Rhee and Sue Chung
Victoria and Oliver Williams
R.J. and Elizabeth Ritter
Felix and Raphael Bommert
Naomi, Duncan and Alistair
Angus and Bobby
Lizzy and Hayden Brandt
Olivia and Emilio
Ace

Francesca Cavallo is an author, activist and entrepreneur. She is the co-author of the New York Times bestselling book series *Good Night Stories for Rebel Girls*. Recipient of the Publisher's Weekly Star Watch Award in 2018, she launched some of the most successful crowdfunding campaigns in the history of publishing, establishing herself as one of the most innovative voices in children's book publishing. In 2019, she founded her second company, Undercats, Inc., with the goal of radically increasing diversity in children's media.

Her books have sold more than five million copies and been translated into over 50 languages.

Instagram: **@francescatherebel**

Claudia Flandoli is a comic book author and a scientific illustrator. She lives and works in the UK where she collaborates with researchers from the University of Cambridge by illustrating their studies.

Instagram: **@claudiaflandoli**

Undercats' books are meant to be conversation-starters. Please let us know what you think about *Doctor Li and the Crown-wearing Virus*: review it online or tag us on Instagram **@undercatsmedia.**

Follow our next releases by signing up on **www.undercats.com**